Articles on the Incas

By

Sir Clements Robert Markham

First published in 1910

Published by Left of Brain Books

Copyright © 2023 Left of Brain Books

ISBN 978-1-397-66481-5

First Edition

All rights reserved. No part of this publication may be reproduced, distributed, or transmitted in any form or by any means, including photocopying, recording, or other electronic or mechanical methods, without the prior written permission of the publisher, except in the case of brief quotations permitted by copyright law. Left of Brain Books is a division of Left Of Brain Onboarding Pty Ltd.

PUBLISHER'S PREFACE

About the Book

Some extracts from historical accounts of the religion of the Inca Empire. The Shepherd And The Daughter Of The Sun, Viracocha And The Coming Of The Incas, Death Of Pachacuti Inca Yupanqui, The Festival of The Sun, and Three Inca Prayers.

About the Author

Sir Clements Robert Markham (1830 - 1916)

"Sir Clements Robert Markham KCB FRS (20 July 1830 - 30 January 1916) was an English explorer, author and geographer. As President of the Royal Geographical Society in the late nineteenth century, Markham was instrumental in financing British exploration of the polar areas. His attempts to have the British be the first to reach the poles, however, ultimately ended in failure.

Markham was born in Stillingfleet, Yorkshire, England. He was educated at Westminster School, joined the Royal Navy in 1844, and became a midshipman in 1848. He was a member of a crew sent to search for John Franklin in 1850, the explorer lost searching for a Northwest Passage in 1845, although few expected to find Franklin alive by this time, given the failure of previous rescue missions. On his return Markham was promoted to lieutenant but resigned from the Navy in 1852.

Following his retirement Markham explored the forests of the eastern Andes in Peru and is credited with introducing the cinchona tree (a source of quinine) to India and other British colonies. Markham inspected the cinchona plantations of Ceylon (now Sri Lanka) and India in 1865-1866. These plantings resulted in the first effective treatment for malaria to be produced within the boundaries of the British Empire. In gratitude for this work, Markham was honored with a knighthood, becoming Sir Clements."

(Quote from wikipedia.org)

CONTENTS

PUBLISHER'S PREFACE
   THE SHEPHERD AND THE DAUGHTER OF THE SUN 1
   VIRACOCHA AND THE COMING OF THE INCAS 7
   DEATH OF PACHACUTI INCA YUPANQUI 32
   THE FESTIVAL OF THE SUN 34
   THREE INCA PRAYERS 55

THE SHEPHERD AND THE DAUGHTER OF THE SUN

From "The Incas of Peru" by Sir Clements Markham, London, Smith Elder & Co. 1910 pp. 408-415

IN THE SNOW-CLAD CORDILLERA above the valley of Yucay, called Pitu-siray, a shepherd watched the flock of white llamas intended for the Inca to sacrifice to the Sun. He was a native of Laris, named Acoya-napa, a very well disposed and gentle youth. He strolled behind his flock, and presently began to play upon his flute very softly and sweetly, neither feeling anything of the amorous desires of youth, nor knowing anything of them.

He was carelessly playing his flute one day when two daughters of the Sun came to him. They could wander in all directions over the green meadows, and never failed to find one of their houses at night, where the guards and porters looked out that nothing came that could do them harm. Well! the two girls came to the place where the shepherd rested quite at his ease, and they asked him about his llamas.

The shepherd, who had not seen them until they spoke, was surprised, and fell on his knees, thinking that they were the embodiments of two out of the four crystalline fountains which were very famous in those parts. So he did not dare to answer them. They repeated their question about the flock, and told him not to be afraid, for they were children of the Sun, who was lord of all the land, and to give him confidence they took him by the arm. Then the shepherd stood up and kissed their hands.

After talking together for some time the shepherd said that it was time for him to collect his flock, and asked their permission. The elder princess, named Chuqui-llantu, had been struck by the grace and good disposition of the shepherd. She asked him his name and of what place he was a native. He replied that his home was at Laris and that his name was Acoya-napa. While he was speaking Chuqui-llantu cast her eyes upon a plate of silver which the shepherd wore over his forehead, and which shone and glittered very prettily. Looking closer she saw on it two figures, very subtilely contrived, who were eating a heart. Chuqui-llantu asked the shepherd the name of that silver ornament, and he said it was called utusi. The princess returned it to the shepherd, and took leave of him, carrying well in her memory the name of the ornament and the figures, thinking with what delicacy they were drawn, almost seeming to her to be alive. She talked about it with her sister until they came to their palace. On entering, the doorkeepers looked to see if they brought with them anything that would do harm, because it was often found that women had brought with them, hidden in their clothes, such things as fillets and necklaces. After having looked well, the porters let them pass, and they found the women of the Sun cooking and preparing food. Chuqui-llantu said that she was very tired with her walk, and that she did not want any supper. All the rest supped with her sister, who thought that Acoya-napa was not one who could cause inquietude. But Chuqui-llantu was unable to rest owing to the great love she felt for the shepherd Acoya-napa, and she regretted that she had not shown him what was in her breast. But at last she went to sleep.

In the palace there were many richly furnished apartments in which the women of the Sun dwelt. These virgins were brought from all the four provinces which were subject to the Inca, namely Chincha-suyu, Cunti-suyu, Anti-suyu and Colla-suyu. Within, there were four fountains which flowed towards the four provinces, and in which the women bathed, each in the fountain of the province where she was born. They named the fountains in this way. That of Chincha-suyu was called Chuclla-puquio, that of Cunti-suyu was known as Ocoruro-puquio, Siclla-puquio was the fountain of Anti-suyu, and Llulucha-puquio of Colla-suyu. The most beautiful child of the Sun, Chuqui-llantu, was wrapped in profound sleep. She had a dream. She thought she saw a bird flying from one tree to another, and singing very softly and sweetly. After having sung for some time, the bird came down and regarded the princess, saying that she should feel no sorrow, for all would be well. The princess said that she mourned for something for which there could be no remedy. The singing bird replied that it would find a remedy, and asked the princess to tell her the cause of her sorrow. At last Chuqui-llantu told the bird of the great love she felt for the shepherd boy named Acoya-napa, who guarded the white flock. Her death seemed inevitable. She could have no cure but to go to him whom she so dearly loved, and if she did her father the Sun would order her to be killed. The answer of the singing bird, by name Checollo, was that she should arise and sit between the four fountains. There she was to sing what she had most in her memory. If the fountains repeated her words, she might then safely do what she wanted. Saying this the bird flew away, and the princess awoke. She was terrified. But she dressed very quickly and put herself between the four fountains. She began to repeat what she remembered to have seen of the two figures on the silver plate, singing:

"Micuc isutu cuyuc utusi cucim."

Presently all the fountains began to sing the same verse.

Seeing that all the fountains were very favourable, the princess went to repose for a little while, for all night she had been conversing with the checollo in her dream.

When the shepherd boy went to his home he called to mind the great beauty of Chuqui-llantu. She had aroused his love, but he was saddened by the thought that it must be love without hope. He took up his flute and played such heart-breaking music that it made him shed many tears, and he lamented, saying: "Ay! ay! ay! for the unlucky and sorrowful shepherd, abandoned and without hope, now approaching the day of your death, for there can be no remedy and no hope." Saying this, he also went to sleep.

The shepherd's mother lived in Laris, and she knew, by her power of divination, the cause of the extreme grief into which her son was plunged, and that he must die unless she took order for providing a remedy. So she set out for the mountains, and arrived at the shepherd's hut at sunrise. She looked in and saw her son almost moribund, with his face covered with tears. She went in and awoke him. When he saw who it was he began to tell her the cause of his grief, and she did what she could to console him. She told him not to be downhearted, because she would find a remedy within a few days. Saying this she departed and, going among the rocks, she gathered certain herbs which are believed to be cures for grief. Having collected a great quantity she began to cook them, and the cooking was not finished before the two princesses appeared at the entrance of the hut. For Chuqui-llantu, when she was rested, had set out with her sister for a walk on the green slopes of the mountains, taking the direction of the hut. Her tender heart prevented her from going in any other direction. When they arrived they were tired, and sat down by the entrance. Seeing an old dame inside they saluted her, and asked her if she could give them anything to eat. The mother went down on her knees and said she had nothing but a dish of herbs. She brought it to them, and they began to eat with excellent appetites. Chuqui-llantu then walked round the hut without finding what she sought, for the shepherd's mother had made Acoya-napa lie down inside the hut, under a cloak. So the princess thought that he had gone after his flock. Then she saw the cloak and told the mother that it was a very pretty cloak, asking where it came from. The old woman told her that it was a cloak which, in ancient times, belonged to a woman beloved by Pachacamac, a deity very celebrated in the valleys on the coast. She said it had come to her by inheritance; but the princess, with many endearments, begged for it until at last the mother consented. When Chuqui-llantu took it into her hands she liked it better than before and, after staying a short time longer in the hut, she took leave of the old woman, and walked along the meadows looking about in hopes of seeing him whom she longed for.

We do not treat further of the sister, as she now drops out of the story, but only of Chuqui-llantu. She was very sad and pensive when she could see no signs of her beloved shepherd on her way back to the palace. She was in great sorrow at not having seen him, and when, as was usual, the guards looked at what she brought, they saw nothing but the cloak. A splendid supper was provided, and when every one went to bed the princess took the cloak and placed it at her bedside. As soon as she was alone she began to weep, thinking of the shepherd. She fell asleep at last, but it was not long before the cloak was changed into the being it had been before. It began to call Chuqui-llantu by her own name. She was terribly frightened, got out of bed, and beheld the shepherd on his knees before her, shedding many tears. She was satisfied on seeing him, and inquired how he had got inside the palace. He replied that the cloak which she carried had arranged about that. then Chuqui-llantu embraced him, and put her finely worked lipi mantles on him, and they slept together. When they wanted to get up in the morning, the shepherd again became the cloak. As soon as the sun rose, the princess left the palace of her father with the cloak, and when she reached a ravine in the mountains, she found herself again with her beloved shepherd, who had been changed into himself. But one of the guards had followed them, and when he saw what had happened he gave the alarm with loud shouts. The lovers fled into the mountains which are near the town of Calca. Being tired after a long journey, they climbed to the top of a rock and went to sleep. They heard a great noise in their sleep, so they arose. The princess took one shoe in her hand and kept the other on her foot. Then looking towards the town of Calca both were turned into stone. To this day the two statues may be seen between Calca and Huayllapampa.

VIRACOCHA AND THE COMING OF THE INCAS

From "History of the Incas" by Pedro Sarmiento De Gamboa, translated by Clements Markham, Cambridge: The Hakluyt Society 1907, pp. 28-58

THE NATIVES OF THIS LAND affirm that in the beginning, and before this world was created, there was a being called Viracocha. He created a dark world without sun, moon or stars. Owing to this creation he was named Viracocha Pachayachachi, which means "Creator of all things." And when he had created the world he formed a race of giants of disproportioned greatness painted and sculptured, to see whether it would be well to make real men of that size. He then created men in his likeness as they are now; and they lived in darkness.

Viracocha ordered these people that they should live without quarrelling, and that they should know and serve him. He gave them a certain precept which they were to observe on pain of being confounded if they should break it. They kept this precept for some time, but it is not mentioned what it was. But as there arose among them the vices of pride and covetousness, they transgressed the precept of Viracocha Pachayachachi and falling, through this sin, under his indignation, he confounded and cursed them. Then some were turned into stones, others into other things, some were swallowed up by the earth, others by the sea, and over all there came a general flood which they call uñu pachacuti, which means "water that overturns the land." They say that it rained 60 days and nights, that it drowned all created things, and that there alone remained some vestiges of those who were turned into stones, as a memorial of the event, and as an example to posterity, in the edifices of Pucara, which are 60 leagues from Cuzco.

Some of the nations, besides the Cuzcos, also say that a few were saved from this flood to leave descendants for a future age. Each nation has its special fable which is told by its people, of how their first ancestors were saved from the waters of the deluge. That the ideas they had in their blindness may be understood, I will insert only one, told by the nation of the Cañaris, a land of Quito and Tumibamba, 400 leagues from Cuzco and more.

They say that in the time of the deluge called uñu pachacuti there was a mountain named Guasano in the province of Quito and near a town called Tumipampa. The natives still point it out. Up this mountain went two of the Cañaris named Ataorupagui and Cusicayo. As the waters increased the mountain kept rising and keeping above them in such a way that it was never covered by the waters of the flood. In this way the two Cañaris escaped. These two, who were brothers, when the waters abated after the flood, began to sow. One day when they had been at work, on returning to their but, they found in it some small loaves of bread, and a jar of chicha, which is the beverage used in this country in place of wine, made of boiled maize. They did not know who had brought it, but they gave thanks to the Creator, eating and drinking of that provision. Next day the same thing happened. As they marvelled at this mystery, they were anxious to find out who brought the meals. So one day they hid themselves, to spy out the bringers of their food. While they were watching they saw two Cañari women preparing the victuals and putting them in the accustomed place. When about to depart the men tried to seize them, but they evaded their would-be captors and escaped. The Cañaris, seeing the mistake they had made in molesting those who had done them so much good, became sad and prayed to Viracocha for pardon for their sins, entreating him to let the women come back and give them the accustomed meals. The Creator granted their petition. The women came back and said to the Cañaris--"The Creator has thought it well that we should return to you, lest you should die of hunger." They brought them food. Then there was friendship between the women and the Cañari brothers, and one of the Cañari brothers had connexion with one of the women. Then, as the elder brother was drowned in a lake which was near, the survivor married one of the women, and had the other as a concubine. By them he had ten sons who formed two lineages of five each, and increasing in numbers they called one Hanansaya which is the same as to say the upper party, and the other Hurinsaya, or the lower party. From these all the Cañaris that now exist are descended.

In the same way the other nations have fables of how some of their people were saved, from whom they trace their origin and descent. But the Incas and most of those of Cuzco, those among them who are believed to know most, do not say that anyone escaped from the flood, but that Viracocha began to create men afresh, as will be related further on. One thing is believed among all the nations of these parts, for they all speak generally and as well known of the general flood which they call uñu pachacuti. From this we may clearly understand that if, in these parts they have a tradition of the great flood, this great mass of the floating islands which they afterwards called the Atlanticas, and now the Indies of Castille, or America, must have begun to receive a population immediately after the flood, although, by their account, the details are different from those which the true Scriptures teach us. This must have been done by divine Providence, through the first people coming over the land of the Atlantic Island, which was joined to this, as has been already said. For as the natives, though barbarous, give reasons for their very ancient settlement, by recording the flood, there is no necessity for setting aside the Scriptures by quoting authorities to establish this origin. We now come to those who relate the events of the second age after the flood, which is the subject of the next chapter.

FABLE OF THE SECOND AGE, AND CREATION OF THE BARBAROUS INDIANS ACCORDING TO THEIR ACCOUNT

IT IS RELATED that everything was destroyed in the flood called uñu pachacuti. It must now be known that Viracocha Pachayachachi, when he destroyed that land as has been already recounted, preserved three men, one of them named Taguapaca, that they might serve and help him in the creation of new people who had to be made in the second age after the deluge, which was done in this manner. The flood being passed and the land dry, Viracocha determined to people it a second time, and, to make it more perfect, he decided upon creating luminaries to give it light. With this object he went, with his servants, to a great lake in the Collao, in which there is an island called Titicaca, the meaning being "the rock of lead," of which we shall treat in the first part. Viracocha went to this island, and presently ordered that the sun, moon, and stars should come forth, and be set in the heavens to give light to the world, and it was so. They say that the moon was created brighter than the sun, which made the sun jealous at the time when they rose into the sky. So the sun threw over the moon's face a handful of ashes, which gave it the shaded colour it now presents. This frontier lake of Chucuito, in the territory of the Collao, is 57 leagues to the south of Cuzco. Viracocha gave various orders to his servants, but Taguapaca disobeyed the commands of Viracocha. So Viracocha was enraged against Taguapaca, and ordered the other two servants to take him, tie him hands and feet, and launch him in a balsa on the lake. This was done. Taguapaca was blaspheming against Viracocha for the way he was treated, and threatening that he would return and take vengeance, when he was carried by the water down the drain of the same lake, and was not seen again for a long time. This done, Viracocha made a sacred idol in that place, as a place for worship and as a sign of what he had there created.

Leaving the island, he passed by the lake to the main land, taking with him the two servants who survived. He went to a place now called Tiahuanacu in the province of Collasuyu, and in this place he sculptured and designed on a great piece of stone, all the nations that he intended to create. This done, he ordered his two servants to charge their memories with the names of all tribes that he had depicted, and of the valleys and provinces where they were to come forth, which were those of the whole land. He ordered that each one should go by a different road, naming the tribes, and ordering them all to go forth and people the country. His servants, obeying the command of Viracocha, set out on their journey and work. One went by the mountain range or chain which they call the heights over the plains on the South Sea. The other went by the heights which overlook the wonderful mountain ranges which we call the Andes, situated to the east of the said sea. By these roads they went, saying with a loud voice "Oh you tribes and nations, hear and obey the order of Ticci Viracocha Pachayachachi, which commands you to go forth, and multiply and settle the land." Viracocha himself did the same along the road between those taken by his two servants, naming all the tribes and places by which he passed. At the sound of his voice every place obeyed, and people came forth, some from lakes, others from fountains, valleys, caves, trees, rocks and hills, spreading over the land and multiplying to form the nations which are to-day in Peru.

Others affirm that this creation of Viracocha was made from the Titicaca site where, having originally formed some shapes of large strong men which seemed to him out of proportion, he made them again of his stature which was, as they say, the average height of men, and being made he gave them life. Thence they set out to people the land. As they spoke one language previous to starting, they built those edifices, the ruins of which may still be seen, before they set out. This was for the residence of Viracocha, their maker. After departing they varied their languages, noting the cries of wild beasts, insomuch that, coming across each other afterwards, those could not understand who had before been relations and neighbours.

Whether it was in one way or the other, all agree that Viracocha was the creator of these people. They have the tradition that he was a man of medium height, white and dressed in a white robe like an alb secured round the waist, and that he carried a staff and a book in his hands.

Besides this they tell of a strange event; how that Viracocha, after he had created all people, went on his road and came to a place where many men of his creation had congregated. This place is now called Cacha. When Viracocha arrived there, the inhabitants were estranged owing to his dress and bearing. They murmured at it and proposed to kill him from a hill that was near. They took their weapons there, and gathered together with evil intentions against Viracocha. He, falling on his knees on some plain ground, with his hands clasped, fire from above came down upon those on the hill, and covered all the place, burning up the earth and stones like straw. Those bad men were terrified at the fearful fire. They came down from the hill, and sought pardon from Viracocha for their sin. Viracocha was moved by compassion. He went to the flames and put them out with his staff. But the hill remained quite parched up, the stones being rendered so light by the burning that a very large stone which could not have been carried on a cart, could be raised easily by one man. This may be seen at this day, and it is a wonderful sight to behold this hill, which is a quarter of a league in extent, all burnt up. It is in the Collao.

After this Viracocha continued his journey and arrived at a place called Urcos, 6 leagues to the south of Cuzco. Remaining there some days he was well served by the natives of that neighborhood. At the time of his departure, he made them a celebrated huaca or statue, for them to offer gifts to and worship; to which statue the Incas, in after times, offered many rich gifts of gold and other metals, and above all a golden bench. When the Spaniards entered Cuzco they found it, and appropriated it to themselves. It was worth $17,000. The Marquis Don Francisco Pizarro took it himself, as the share of the General.

Returning to the subject of the fable, Viracocha continued his journey, working his miracles and instructing his created beings. In this way he reached the territory on the equinoctial line, where are now Puerto Viejo and Manta. Here he was joined by his servants. Intending to leave the land of Peru, he made a speech to those he had created, apprising them of the things that would happen. He told them that people would come, who would say that they were Viracocha their creator, and that they were not to believe them; but that in the time to come he would send his messengers who would protect and teach them. Having said this he went to sea with his two servants, and went travelling over the water as if it was land, without sinking. For they appeared like foam over the water, and the people, therefore, gave them the name of Viracocha which is the same as to say the grease or foam of the sea. At the end of some years after Viracocha departed, they say that Taguapaca, whom Viracocha ordered to be thrown into the lake of Titicaca in the Collao, as has already been related, came back and began, with others, to preach that he was Viracocha. Although at first the people were doubtful, they finally saw that it was false, and ridiculed them.

This absurd fable of their creation is held by these barbarians and they affirm and believe it as if they had really seen it to happen and come to pass.

THE ANCIENT FREEDOMS OF THESE KINGDOMS OF PERU AND THEIR PROVINCES

It is important to note that these barbarians could tell nothing more respecting what happened from the second creation by Viracocha down to the time of the Incas. But it may be assumed that, although the land was peopled and full of inhabitants before the Incas, it had no regular government, nor did it have natural lords elected by common consent to govern and rule, and who were respected by the people, so that they were obeyed and received tribute. On the contrary all the people were scattered and disorganized, living in complete liberty, and each man being sole lord of his house and estate. In each tribe there were two divisions. One was called Hanansaya, which means the upper division, and the other Hurinsaya, which is the lower division, a custom which continues to this day. These divisions do not mean anything more than a way to count each other, for their satisfaction; though afterwards it served a more useful purpose, as will be seen in its place.

As there were dissensions among them, a certain kind of militia was organized for defence, in the following way. When it became known to the people of one district that some from other parts were coming to make war, they chose one who was a native, or he might be a stranger, who was known to be a valiant warrior. Often such a man offered himself to aid and to fight for them against their enemies. Such a man was followed and his orders were obeyed during the war. When the war was over he became a private man as he had been before, like the rest of the people, nor did they pay him tribute either before or afterwards, nor any manner of tax whatever. To such a man they gave and still give the name of Sinchi which means valiant. They call such men "Sinchi-cuna" which means "valiant now" as who should say--"now during the time the war lasts you shall be our valiant man, and afterwards no": or another meaning would be simply "valiant men," for "cuna" is an adverb of time, and also denotes the plural. In whichever meaning, it is very applicable to these temporary captains in the days of general liberty. So that from the general flood of which they have a tradition to the time when the Incas began to reign, which was 3519 years, all the natives of these kingdoms lived on their properties without acknowledging either a natural or an elected lord. They succeeded in preserving, as it is said, a simple state of liberty, living in huts or caves or humble little houses. This name of Sinchi for those who held sway only during war, lasted throughout the land until the time of Tupac Inca Yupanqui, the tenth Inca, who instituted Curacas and other officials in the order which will be fully described in the life of that Inca. Even at the present time they continue this use and custom in the provinces of Chile and in other parts of the forests of Peru to the east of Quito and Chachapoyas, where they only obey a chief during war time, not any special one, but he who is known to be most valiant, enterprising and daring in the wars. The reader should note that all the land was private property with reference to any dominion of chiefs, yet they had natural chiefs with special rights in each province, as for instance among the natives of the valley of Cuzco and in other parts, as we shall relate of each part in its place.

THE FIRST SETTLERS IN THE VALLEY OF CUZCO

I have explained how the people of these lands preserved their inheritances and lived on them in ancient times, and that their proper and natural countries were known. There were many of these which I shall notice in their places, treating specially at present of the original settlers of the valley where stands the present city of Cuzco. For from there we have to trace the origin of the tyranny of the Incas, who always had their chief seat in the valley of Cuzco.

Before all things it must be understood that the valley of Cuzco is in 13° 15' from the equator on the side of the south pole. In this valley, owing to its being fertile for cultivation, there were three tribes settled from most ancient times, the first called Sauaseras, the second Antasayas, the third Huallas. They settled near each other, although their lands for sowing were distinct, which is the property they valued most in those days and even now. These natives of the valley lived there in peace for many years, cultivating their farms.

Some time before the arrival of the Incas, three Sinchis, strangers to this valley, the first named Alcabisa, the second Copalimayta, and the third Culunchima, collected certain companies and came to the valley of Cuzco, where, by consent of the natives, they settled and became brothers and companions of the original inhabitants. So they lived for a long time. There was concord between these six tribes, three native and three immigrant. They relate that the immigrants came out to where the Incas then resided, as we shall relate presently, and called them relations. This is an important point with reference to what happened afterwards.

Before entering upon the history of the Incas I wish to make known or, speaking more accurately, to answer a difficulty which may occur to those who have not been in these parts. Some may say that this history cannot be accepted as authentic being taken from the narratives of these barbarians, because, having no letters, they could not preserve such details as they give from so remote an antiquity. The answer is that, to supply the want of letters, these barbarians had a curious invention which was very good and accurate. This was that from one to the other, from fathers to sons, they handed down past events, repeating the story of them many times, just as lessons are repeated from a professor's chair, making the hearers say these historical lessons over and over again until they were fixed in the memory. Thus each one of the descendants continued to communicate the annals in the order described with a view to preserve their histories and deeds, their ancient traditions, the numbers of their tribes, towns, provinces, their days, months and years, their battles, deaths, destructions, fortresses and Sinchis. Finally they recorded, and they still record, the most notable things which may be expressed in numbers (or statistics), on certain cords called quipu, which is the same as to say reasoner or accountant. On these cords they make certain knots by which, and by differences of colour, they distinguish and record each thing as by letters. It is a thing to be admired to see what details may be recorded on these cords, for which there are masters like our writing masters.

Besides this they had, and still have, special historians in these nations, an hereditary office descending from father to son. The collection of these annals is due to the great diligence of Pachacuti Inca Yupanqui, the ninth Inca, who sent out a general summons to an the old historians in all the provinces he had subjugated, and even to many others throughout those kingdoms. He had them in Cuzco for a long time, examining them concerning their antiquities, origin, and the most notable events in their history. These were painted on great boards, and deposited in the temple of the Sun, in a great hall. There such boards, adorned with gold, were kept as in our libraries, and learned persons were appointed, who were well versed in the art of understanding and declaring their contents. No one was allowed to enter where these boards were kept, except the Inca and the historians, without a special order of the Inca.

In this way they took care to have all their past history investigated, and to have records respecting all kinds of people, so that at this day the Indians generally know and agree respecting details and important events, though, in some things, they hold different opinions on special points. By examining the oldest and most prudent among them, in all ranks of life, who had most credit, I collected and compiled the present history, referring the sayings and declarations of one party to their antagonists of another party, for they are divided into parties, and seeking from each one a memorial of its lineage and of that of the opposing party. These memorials, which are all in my possession, were compared and corrected, and ultimately verified in public, in presence of representatives of all the parties and lineages, under oaths in presence of a judge, and with expert and very faithful interpreters also on oath, and I thus finished what is now written. Such great diligence has been observed, because the facts which will be obvious on the true completion of such a great work-the establishment of the tyranny of the cruel Incas of this land-will make all the nations of the world understand the judicial and more than legitimate right that the King of Castille has to these Indies and to other lands adjacent, especially to these kingdoms of Peru. As all the histories of past events have been verified by proof, which in this case has been done so carefully and faithfully by order and owing to the industry of the most excellent Viceroy Don Francisco de Toledo, no one can doubt that everything in this volume is most sufficiently established and verified without any room being left for reply or contradiction. I have been desirous of making this digression because, in writing the history, I have heard that many entertain the doubts I have above referred to, and it seemed well to satisfy them once for all.

HOW THE INCAS BEGAN TO TYRANNIZE OVER THE LANDS AND INHERITANCES

Having explained that, in ancient times, all this land was owned by the people, it is necessary to state how the Incas began their tyranny. Although the tribes all lived in simple liberty without recognising any lord, there were always some ambitious men among them, aspiring for mastery. They committed violence among their countrymen and among strangers to subject them and bring them to obedience under their command, so that they might serve them and pay tribute. Thus bands of men belonging to one region went to others to make war and to rob and kill, usurping the lands of others.

As these movements took place in many parts by many tribes, each one trying to subjugate his neighbour, it happened that 6 leagues from the valley of Cuzco, at a place called Paccari-tampu, there were four men with their four sisters, of fierce courage and evil intentions, although with lofty aims. These, being more able than the others, understood the pusillanimity of the natives of those districts and the ease with which they could be made to believe anything that was propounded with authority or with any force. So they conceived among themselves the idea of being able to subjugate many lands by force and deception. Thus all the eight brethren, four men and four women, consulted together how they could tyrannize over other tribes beyond the place where they lived, and they proposed to do this by violence. Considering that most of the natives were ignorant and could easily be made to believe what was said to them, particularly if they were addressed with some roughness, rigour and authority, against which they could make neither reply nor resistance because they are timid by nature, they sent abroad certain fables respecting their origin, that they might be respected and feared. They said that they were the sons of Viracocha Pachayachachi, the Creator, and that they had come forth out of certain windows to rule the rest of the people. As they were fierce, they made the people believe and fear them, and hold them to be more than men, even worshipping them as gods. Thus they introduced the religion that suited them. The order of the fable they told of their origin was as follows.

THE FABLE OF THE ORIGIN OF THE INCAS OF CUZCO

All the native Indians of this land relate and affirm that the Incas Ccapac originated in this way. Six leagues S.S.W. of Cuzco by the road which the Incas made, there is a place called Paccari-tampu, at which there is a hill called Tampu-tocco, meaning "the house of windows." It is certain that in this hill there are three windows, one called "Maras-tocco," the other "Sutic-tocco," while that which is in the middle, between these two, was known as "Ccapac-tocco," which means "the rich window," because they say that it was ornamented with gold and other treasures. From the window called "Maras-tocco" came forth, without parentage, a tribe of Indians called Maras. There are still some of them in Cuzco. From the "Sutic-tocco" came Indians called Tampus, who settled round the same hill, and there are also men of this lineage still in Cuzco. From the chief window of "Ccapac-tocco," came four men and four women, called brethren. These knew no father nor mother, beyond the story they told that they were created and came out of the said window by order of Ticci Viracocha, and they declared that Viracocha created them to be lords. For this reason they took the name of Inca, which is the same as lord. They took "Ccapac" as an additional name because they came out of the window

"Ccapac-tocco," which means "rich," although afterwards they used this term to denote the chief lord over many.

The names of the eight brethren were as follows: The eldest of the men, and the one with the most authority was named Manco Ccapac, the second Ayar Auca, the third Ayar Cachi, the fourth Ayar Uchu. Of the women the eldest was called Mama Occlo, the second Mama Huaco, the third Mama Ipacura, or, as others say, Mama Cura, the fourth Mama Raua.

The eight brethren, called Incas, said--"We are born strong and wise, and with the people who will here join us, we shall be powerful. We will go forth from this place to seek fertile lands and when we find them we will subjugate the people and take the lands, making war on all those who do not receive us as their lords." This, as they relate, was said by Mama Huaco, one of the women, who was fierce and cruel. Manco Ccapac, her brother, was also cruel and atrocious. This being agreed upon between the eight, they began to move the people who lived near the hill, putting it to them that their reward would be to become rich and to receive the lands and estates of those who were conquered and subjugated. For these objects they moved ten tribes or ayllus, which means among these barbarians "lineages" or "parties"; the names of which are as follows:

I. Chauin Cuzco Ayllu of the lineage of Ayar Cachi, of which there are still some in Cuzco, the chiefs being Martin Chucumbi, and Don Diego Huaman Paucar.

II. Arayraca Ayllu Cuzco-Callan. At present there are of this ayllu Juan Pizarro Yupanqui, Don Francisco Quispi, Alonso Tarma Yupanqui of the lineage of Ayar Uchu.

III. Tarpuntay Ayllu. Of this there are now some in Cuzco.

IV. Huacaytaqui Ayllu. Some still living in Cuzco.

V. Sañoc Ayllu. Some still in Cuzco. The above five lineages are Hanan-Cuzco, which means the party of Upper Cuzco.

VI. Sutic-Tocco Ayllu is the lineage which came out of one of the windows called "Sutic-Tocco," as has been before explained. Of these there are still some in Cuzco, the chiefs being Don Francisco Avca Micho Avri Sutic, and Don Alonso Hualpa.

VII. Maras Ayllu. These are of the men who came forth from the window "Maras-Tocco." There are some of these now in Cuzco, the chiefs being Don Alonso Llama Oca, and Don Gonzalo Ampura Llama Oca.

VIII. Cuycusa Ayllu. Of these there are still some in Cuzco, the chief being Cristoval Acllari.

IX. Masca Ayllu. Of this there is in Cuzco, Juan Quispi.

X. Oro Ayllu. Of this lineage is Don Pedro Yucay.

I say that all these ayllus have preserved their records in such a way that the memory of them has not been lost. There are more of them than are given above, for I only insert the chiefs who are the protectors and heads of the lineages, under whose guidance they are preserved. Each chief has the duty and obligation to protect the rest, and to know the history of his ancestors. Although I say that these live in Cuzco, the truth is that they are in a suburb of the city which the Indians call Cayocache and which is known to us as Belem, from the church of that parish which is that of our Lady of Belem.

Returning to our subject, all these followers above-mentioned marched with Manco Ccapac and the other brethren to seek for land (and to tyrannize over those who did no harm to them, nor gave them any excuse for war, and without any right or title beyond what has been stated). To be prepared for war they chose for their leaders Manco Ccapac and Mama Huaco, and with this arrangement the companies of the hill of Tampu-tocco set out, to put their design into execution.

THE ROAD WHICH THESE COMPANIES OF THE INCAS TOOK TO THE VALLEY OF CUZCO, AND OF THE FABLES WHICH ARE MIXED WITH THEIR HISTORY

The Incas and the rest of the companies or ayllus set out from their homes at Tampu-tocco, taking with them their property and arms, in sufficient numbers to form a good squadron, having for their chiefs the said Manco Ccapac and Mama Huaco.

Manco Ccapac took with him a bird like a falcon, called indi, which they all worshipped and feared as a sacred, or, as some say, an enchanted thing, for they thought that this bird made Manco Ccapac their lord and obliged the people to follow him. It was thus that Manco Ccapac gave them to understand, and it was always kept in a covered hamper of straw, like a box, with much care. He left it as an heirloom to his son, and the Incas had it down to the time of Inca Yupanqui. In his hand he carried with him a staff of gold, to test the lands which they would come to.

Marching together they came to a place called Huanacancha, four leagues from the valley of Cuzco, where they remained for some time, sowing and seeking for fertile land. Here Manco Ccapac had connection with his sister Mama Occlo, and she became pregnant by him. As this place did not appear able to sustain them, being barren, they advanced to another place called Tampu-quiro, where Mama Occlo begot a son named Sinchi Rocca. Having celebrated the natal feasts of the infant, they set out in search of fertile land, and came to another place called Pallata, which is almost contiguous to Tampu-quiro, and there they remained for some years.

Not content with this land, they came to another called Haysquisro, a quarter of a league further on. Here they consulted together over what ought to be done respecting their journey, and over the best way of getting rid of Ayar Cachi, one of the four brothers. Ayar Cachi was fierce and strong, and very dexterous with the sling. He committed great cruelties and was oppressive both among the natives of the places they passed, and among his own people. The other brothers were afraid that the conduct of Ayar Cachi would cause their companies to disband and desert, and that they would be left alone. As Manco Ccapac was prudent, he concurred with the opinion of the others that they should secure their object by deceit. They called Ayar Cachi and said to him, "Brother! Know that in Ccapac-tocco we have forgotten the golden vases called tupac-cusi, and certain seeds, and the napa, which is our principal ensign of sovereignty." The napa is a sheep of the country, the colour white, with a red body cloth, on the top ear-rings of gold, and on the breast a plate with red badges such as was worn by rich Incas when they went abroad; carried in front of all on a pole with a cross of plumes of feathers. This was called suntur-paucar. They said that it would be for the good of all, if he would go back and fetch them. When Ayar Cachi refused to return, his sister Mama Huaco, raising her foot, rebuked him with furious words, saying, "How is it that there should be such cowardice in so strong a youth as you are? Get ready for the journey, and do not fail to go to Tampu-tocco, and do what you are ordered." Ayar Cachi was shamed by these words. He obeyed and started to carry out his orders. They gave him, as a companion, one of those who had come with them, named Tampu-chacay, to whom they gave secret orders to kill Ayar Cachi at Tampu-tocco, and not to return with him. With these orders they both arrived at Tampu-tocco. They had scarcely arrived when Ayar Cachi entered through the window Ccapac-tocco, to get the things for which he had been sent. He was no sooner inside than Tampu-chacay, with great celerity, put a rock against the opening of the window and sat upon it, that Ayar Cachi might remain inside and die there. When Ayar Cachi turned to the opening and found it closed he understood the treason of which the traitor Tampu-chacay had been guilty, and determined to get out if it was possible, to take vengeance. To force an opening he used such force and shouted so loud that he made the mountain tremble. With a loud voice he spoke these words to Tampu-chacay, "Thou traitor! thou who hast done me so much harm, thinkest thou to convey the news of my mortal imprisonment? That shall, never happen. For thy treason thou shalt remain outside, turned into a stone." So it was done, and to this day they show the stone on one side of the window Ccapac-tocco. Turn we now to the seven brethren who had remained at Hays-quisro. The death of Ayar Cachi being known, they were very sorry for what they had done, for, as he was valiant, they regretted much to be without him when the time came to make war on any one. So they mourned for him. This Ayar Cachi was so dexterous with a sling and so strong that with each shot he pulled down a mountain and filled up a ravine. They say that the ravines, which we now see on their line of march, were made by Ayar Cachi in hurling stones.

The seven Incas and their companions left this place, and came to another called Quirirmanta at the foot of a hill which was afterwards called Huanacauri. In this place they consulted together how they should divide the duties of the enterprise amongst themselves, so that there should be distinctions between them. They agreed that as Manco Ccapac had had a child by his sister, they should be married and have children to continue the lineage, and that he should be the leader. Ayar Uchu was to remain as a huaca for the sake of religion. Ayar Auca, from the position they should select, was to take possession of the land set apart for him to people.

Leaving this place they came to a hill at a distance of two leagues, a little more or less, from Cuzco. Ascending the hill they saw a rainbow, which the natives call huanacauri. Holding it to be a fortunate sign, Manco Ccapac said: "Take this for a sign that the world will not be destroyed by water. We shall arrive and from hence we shall select where we shall found our city." Then, first casting lots, they saw that the signs were good for doing so, and for exploring the land from that point and becoming lords of it. Before they got to the height where the rainbow was, they saw a huaca which was a place of worship in human shape, near the rainbow. They determined among themselves to seize it and take it away from there. Ayar Uchu offered himself to go to it, for they said that he was very like it. When Ayar Uchu came to the statue or huaca, with great courage he sat upon it, asking it what it did there. At these words the huaca turned its head to see who spoke, but, owing to the weight upon it, it could not see. Presently, when Ayar Uchu wanted to get off he was not able, for he found that the soles of his feet were fastened to the shoulders of the huaca. The six brethren, seeing that he was a prisoner, came to succour him. But Ayar Uchu, finding himself thus transformed, and that his brethren could not release him, said to them--"O Brothers, an evil work you have wrought for me. It was for your sakes that I came where I must remain for ever, apart from your company. Go! go! happy brethren. I announce to you that you will be great lords. I, therefore, pray that in recognition of the desire I have always had to please you, you will honour and venerate me in all your festivals and ceremonies, and that I shall be the first to whom you make offerings. For I remain here for your sakes. When you celebrate the huarachico (which is the arming of the sons as knights) you shall adore me as their father, for I shall remain here for ever." Manco Ccapac answered that he would do so, for that it was his will and that it should be so ordered. Ayar Uchu promised for the youths that he would bestow on them the gifts of valour, nobility, and knighthood, and with these last words he remained, turned into stone. They constituted him the huaca of the Incas, giving it the name of Ayar Uchu Huanacauri. And so it always was, until the arrival of the Spaniards, the most venerated huaca, and the one that received the most offerings of any in the kingdom. Here the Incas went to arm the young knights until about twenty years ago, when the Christians abolished this ceremony. It was religiously done, because there were many abuses and idolatrous practices, offensive and contrary to the ordinances of God our Lord.

ENTRY OF THE INCAS INTO THE VALLEY OF CUZCO, AND THE FABLES THEY RELATE CONCERNING IT

The six brethren were sad at the loss of Ayar Uchu, and at the loss of Ayar Cachi; and, owing to the death of Ayar Cachi, those of the lineage of the Incas, from that time to this day, always fear to go to Tampu-tocco, lest they should have to remain there like Ayar Cachi.

They went down to the foot of the hill, whence they began their entry into the valley of Cuzco, arriving at a place called Matahua, where they stopped and built huts, intending to remain there some time. Here they armed as knight the son of Manco Ccapac and of Mama Occlo, named Sinchi Rocca, and they bored his ears, a ceremony which is called huarachico, being the insignia of his knighthood and nobility, like the custom known among ourselves. On this occasion they indulged in great rejoicings, drinking for many days, and at intervals mourning for the loss of their brother Ayar Uchu. It was here that they invented the mourning sound for the dead, like the cooing of a dove. Then they performed the dance called Ccapac Raymi, a ceremony of the royal or great lords. It is danced, in long purple robes, at the ceremonies they call quicochico, which is when girls come to maturity, and the huarachico, when they pierce the ears of the Incas, and the rutuchico, when the Inca's hair is cut the first time, and the ayuscay, which is when a child is born, and they drink continuously for four or five days.

After this they were in Matahua for two years, waiting to pass on to the upper valley to seek good and fertile land. Mama Huaco, who was very strong and dexterous, took two wands of gold and hurled them towards the north. One fell, at two shots of an arquebus, into a ploughed field called Colcapampa and did not drive in well, the soil being loose and not terraced. By this they knew that the soil was not fertile. The other went further, to near Cuzco, and fixed well in the territory called Huanay-pata, where they knew the land to be fertile. Others say that this proof was made by Manco Ccapac with the staff of gold which he carried himself, and that thus they knew of the fertility of the land, when the staff sunk in the land called Huanay-pata, two shots of an arquebus from Cuzco. They knew the crust of the soil to be rich and close, so that it could only be broken by using much force.

Let it be by one way or the other, for all agree that they went trying the land with a pole or staff until they arrived at this Huanay-pata, when they were satisfied. They were sure of its fertility, because after sowing perpetually, it always yielded abundantly, giving more the more it was sown. They determined to usurp that land by force, in spite of the natural owners, and to do with it as they chose. So they returned to Matahua.

From that place Manco Ccapac saw a heap of stones near the site of the present monastery of Santo Domingo at Cuzco. Pointing it out to his brother Ayar Auca, he said, "Brother! you remember how it was arranged between us, that you should go to take possession of the land where we are to settle. Well! look at that stone." Pointing out the stone he continued, "Go thither flying," for they say that Ayar Auca had developed some wings, "and seating yourself there, take possession of land seen from that heap of stones. We will presently come to settle and reside." When Ayar Auca heard the words of his brother, he opened his wings and flew to that place which Manco Ccapac had pointed out. Seating himself there, he was presently turned into stone, and was made the stone of possession. In the ancient language of this valley the heap was called cozco, whence that site has had the name of Cuzco to this day. From this circumstance the Incas had a proverb which said, "Ayar Auca cuzco huanca," or, "Ayar Auca a heap of marble." Others say that Manco Ccapac gave the name of Cuzco because he wept in that place where he buried his brother Ayar Cachi. Owing to his sorrow and to the fertility, he gave that name which in the ancient language of that time signified sad as well as fertile. The first version must be the correct one because Ayar Cachi was not buried at Cuzco, having died at Ccapac-tocco as has been narrated before. And this is generally affirmed by Incas and natives.

Five brethren only remaining, namely Manco Ccapac, and the four sisters, and Manco Ccapac being the only surviving brother out of four, they presently resolved to advance to where Ayar Auca had taken possession. Manco Ccapac first gave to his son Sinchi Rocca a wife named Mama Cuca, of the lineage of Sañu, daughter of a Sinchi named Sitic-huaman, by whom he afterwards had a son named Sapaca. He also instituted the sacrifice called capa cocha, which is the immolation of two male and two female infants before the idol Huanacauri, at the time when the Incas were armed as knights. These things being arranged, he ordered the companies to follow him to the place where Ayar Auca was.

Arriving on the land of Huanay-pata, which is near where now stands the Arco de la plata leading to the Charcas road, he found settled there a nation of Indians named Huallas, already mentioned. Manco Ccapac and Mama Occlo began to settle and to take possession of the land and water, against the will of the Huallas. In this business they did many violent and unjust things. As the Huallas attempted to defend their lives and properties, many cruelties were committed by Manco Ccapac and Mama Occlo. They relate that Mama Occlo was so fierce that, having killed one of the Hualla Indians, she cut him up, took out the inside, carried the heart and lungs in her mouth, and with an ayuinto, which is a stone fastened to a rope, in her hand, she attacked the Huallas with diabolical resolution. When the Huallas beheld this horrible and inhuman spectacle, they feared that the same things would be done to them, being simple and timid, and they fled and abandoned their rights. Mama Occlo reflecting on her cruelty, and fearing that for it they would be branded as tyrants, resolved not to spare any Huallas, believing that the affair would thus be forgotten. So they killed all they could lay their hands upon, dragging infants from their mothers' wombs, that no memory might be left of these miserable Huallas.

Having done this Manco Ccapac advanced, and came within a mile of Cuzco to the S. E., where a Sinchi named Copalimayta came out to oppose him. We have mentioned this chief before and that, although he was a late comer, he settled with the consent of the natives of the valley, and had been incorporated in the nation of Sauaseray Panaca, natives of the site of Santo Domingo at Cuzco. Having seen the strangers invading their lands and tyrannizing over them, and knowing the cruelties inflicted on the Huallas, they had chosen Copalimayta as their Sinchi. He came forth to resist the invasion, saying that the strangers should not enter his lands or those of the natives. His resistance was such that Manco Ccapac and his companions were obliged to turn their backs. They returned to Huanay-pata, the land they had usurped from the Huallas. From the sowing they had made they derived a fine crop of maize, and for this reason they gave the place a name which means something precious.

After some months they returned to the attack on the natives of the valley, to tyrannize over them. They assaulted the settlement of the Sauaseras, and were so rapid in their attack that they captured Copalimayta, slaughtering many of the Sauaseras with great cruelty. Copalimayta, finding himself a prisoner and fearing death, fled out of desperation, leaving his estates, and was never seen again after he escaped. Mama Huaco and Manco Ccapac usurped his houses, lands and people. In this way Manco Ccapac, Mama Huaco, Sinchi Rocca, and Manco Sapaca settled on the site between the two rivers, and erected the House of the Sun, which they called Ynti-cancha. They divided all that position, from Santo Domingo to the junction of the rivers into four neighbourhoods or quarters which they call cancha. They called one Quinti-cancha, the second Chumpi-cancha, the third Sayri-cancha, and the fourth Yarampuy-cancha. They divided the sites among themselves, and thus the city was peopled, and, from the heap of stones of Ayar Auca it was called Cuzco.

DEATH OF PACHACUTI INCA YUPANQUI

From "History of the Incas" by Pedro Sarmiento De Gamboa, translated by Clements Markham, Cambridge: The Hakluyt Society 1907, pp. 138-139

BEING IN THE HIGHEST PROSPERITY and sovereignty of his life, he fell ill of a grave infirmity, and, feeling that he was at the point of death, he sent for all his sons who were then in the city. In their presence he first divided all his jewels and contents of his wardrobe. Next he made them plough furrows in token that they were vassals of their brother, and that they had to eat by the sweat of their hands. He also gave them arms in token that they were to fight for their brother. He then dismissed them.

He next sent for the Incas orejones of Cuzco, his relations, and for Tupac Inca his son to whom he spoke, with a few words, in this manner: "Son! you now see how many great nations I leave to you, and you know what labour they have cost me. Mind that you are the man to keep and augment them. No one must raise his two eyes against you and live, even if he be your own brother. I leave you these our relations that they may be your councillors. Care for them and they shall serve you. When I am dead, take care of my body, and put it in my houses at Patallacta. Have my golden image in the House of the Sun, and make my subjects, in all the provinces, offer up solemn sacrifice, after which keep the feast of purucaya, that I may go to rest with my father the Sun." Having finished his speech they say that he began to sing in a low and sad voice with words of his own language. They are as follows:

"I was born as a flower of the field,
As a flower I was cherished in my youth,
I came to my full age, I grew old,
Now I am withered and die."

Having uttered these words, he laid his head upon a pillow and expired, giving his soul to the devil, having lived a hundred and twenty-five years. For he succeeded, or rather he took the Incaship into his hands when he was twenty-two, and he was sovereign one hundred and three years.

THE FESTIVAL OF THE SUN

From "The First Part of the Royal Commentaries of the Incas" by Garcilaso de la Vega, El Inca, Translated by Sir Clements Markham. London: The Hakluyt Society, First Series #45, 1871. Volume II, pp. 155-167

THE WORD RAYMI is equivalent to our word Easter. Among the four festivals which the Kings celebrated in the city of Cuzco, the most solemn was that in honour of the Sun, during the month of June. It was called Yntip Raymi, which means the "Solemn Feast of the Sun." They called this feast especially Raymi, and though the word was also used for other festivals, this was the Raymi, and took place in the June solstice.

They celebrated this festival of the Sun in acknowledgment that they held and adored Him as the sole and universal God who, by his light and power, creates and sustains all things on earth; and that He was the natural father of the first Ynca Manco Ccapac and of his wife Mama Ocllo Huaco, and of all their descendants, who were sent to this earth for the benefit of all people. For these reasons, as they themselves say, this was their most solemn feast.

There were present at it all the chief captains not then employed in war, and all the Curacas, lords of vassals, from all parts of the empire, not because they were ordered to be present, but because they rejoiced to take part in the solemnities of so great a festival. For, as the ceremonies included the worship of the Sun God and of the Ynca their king, there was no one who did not desire to take part in it. When the Curacas were prevented, by old age or sickness, from being present, or by the public service or the long distance, they sent their sons and brothers, accompanied by the noblest of their kindred, to be at the festival in their place. The Ynca was there in person, if not prevented by absence at the wars or while inspecting the provinces.

The opening ceremonies were performed by the king himself as High Priest; for, although there was always a High Priest of the blood royal, who was legitimate uncle or brother of the Ynca, yet the Ynca himself officiated at this great festival, as first-born of the Sun.

The Curacas came in all the splendour they could afford. Some wore dresses adorned with bezants of gold and silver, and with the same fastened as a circlet round their headdresses. Others came in a costume neither more nor less than that in which Hercules is painted, wrapped in the skins of lions, with the heads fixed over their own. These were the Indians who claimed descent from a lion. Others came attired in the fashion that they paint angels, with great wings of the bird called Cuntur. These wings are black and white, and so long that the Spaniards have often killed birds measuring fourteen feet between the tips of the wings. These are the Indians who declare that they are descended from a Cuntur. The Yuncas came attired in the most hideous masks that can be imagined, and they appeared at the feasts making all sorts of grimaces, like fools and simpletons; and for this purpose they brought instruments in their hands, such as badly-made flutes and tambourines, and pieces of skin, to assist them in their fooleries. Other Curacas wore various costumes to distinguish them, and each different tribe came with the arms with which they fought in war. Some had bows and arrows; others lances, darts, javelins, clubs, slings, axes with short handles, and two-handed axes with long handles.

They brought with them paintings of the deeds they had performed in the service of the Sun and of the Yncas, and also great drums and trumpets, with many musicians to play them. In short, they all came in the best attire they could procure, and attended by the grandest and most imposing retinue their means would admit of.

All prepared themselves for the Raymi of the Sun by a rigorous fast; for, in three days they ate nothing but a little unripe maize, and a few herbs called Chucam, with plain water. During this time no fire was lighted throughout the city, and all men abstained from sleeping with their wives.

After the fast, in the evening before the festival, the Ynca sacrificial Priests prepared the sheep and lambs for sacrifice, and got ready the other offerings of food and drink that were to be offered to the Sun. All these offerings had been provided by the people who came to the feast, not only the Curacas and envoys, but also all their relations, vassals, and servants.

The Women of the Sun were engaged, during the night, in preparing an immense quantity of maize pudding called Canca. This was made up into small round cakes, about the size of an apple. It must be understood that the Indians never ate their corn kneaded and made into bread, except at this feast and at another called Situa, and they did not eat this bread during the whole meal, but only two or three mouthfuls of it at the beginning. Their usual food, in place of bread, was maize toasted or boiled in the grain.

The flour for this bread, especially for what was intended for the Ynca and those of the blood royal, was ground by the chosen virgins of the Sun, who cooked all the other food for this feast; that it might appear to be given rather by the Sun to his children than by his sons to him; and it was therefore prepared by the virgins, as women of the Sun.

Another vast assemblage of women ground the corn and cooked the food for the common people. And though the bread was intended for the people, it was yet prepared with care, because this bread was looked upon as sacred, and was only allowed to be eaten once during the year, on occasion of this feast, which was, among the people, the festival of their festivals.

The necessary preparations having been made, the Ynca came forth at dawn, on the day of the festival, accompanied by all his relations, marching according to their age and dignity. They proceeded to the great square, which was called Huacay-pata. Here they waited for sunrise, all of them being barefooted, and all watching the east with great attention. As soon as the sun appeared, they all bent down resting on their elbows (which, among these Indians, is the same as going down on the knees), with the arms apart and the hands raised. Thus they worshipped, and kissed the air (which with them is the equivalent to kissing the hand or the dress of a Prince in Spain); and they adored with much fervour and devotion, looking upon the Sun as their god and natural father.

The Curacas, not being of the blood royal, assembled in an adjoining square, called the Casi-pata, where they used the same forms of adoration as the Yncas.

Presently the King rose to his feet, the rest being still prostrate, and took two great cups of gold, called aquilla, full of the beverage that they drink. He performed this ceremony as the first-born, in the name of his father, the Sun, and, with the cup in his right hand, invited all his relations to drink. This custom of inviting each other to drink was the usual mode by which superiors showed favour and complacency to inferiors, and by which one friend saluted another.

Having given the invitation to drink, the Ynca emptied the vase in his right hand, which was dedicated to the Sun, into a jar of gold, whence the liquor flowed down a stone conduit of very beautiful masonry from the great square to the temple of the Sun, thus being looked upon as drunk by the deity. From the vase in his left hand the Ynca himself drank, that being his share, and then divided what remained among the other Yncas, pouring it into smaller cups of gold and silver. Gradually the principal vase, which the Ynca held, was emptied; and the partakers thus received such virtue from it as was imparted by its having been sanctified by the Sun or the Ynca, or rather by both together. Each member of the blood royal drank of this liquor. The Curacas in the other square received drinks of the beverage made by the chosen virgins, but not that which had also been sanctified by the Ynca.

This ceremony having been performed, which was but a foretaste of what would have to be drunk afterwards, all went in procession to the temple of the Sun. All took off their shoes, except the King, at two hundred paces before reaching the doors; but the King remained with his shoes on, until he came to the doors. The Ynca and his relations then entered the temple as legitimate children of the deity, and there worshipped the image of the Sun. But the Curacas, being unworthy of so great an honour, remained outside in a large square before the temple doors.

The Ynca offered to the Sun the golden vases with which he had performed the ceremony, and the other members of his family gave their cups to the Ynca priests, who were set apart for that office; for persons who were not priests, even if they were of the royal blood, were not allowed to perform the priestly office. Having offered up the cups of the Yncas, the priests came to the doors to receive those of the Curacas, who took their places according to their seniority as vassals, and presented the gold and silver articles which they had brought from their provinces as offerings to the Sun. These offerings were in the form of sheep, lambs, lizards, toads, serpents, foxes, tigers, lions, and many sorts of birds, in short, of all the animals in the provinces, each imitated from nature in gold and silver, though the size of each article was not great.

As soon as the offerings were made, the chiefs returned to their places in procession; and presently the priests came out with many lambs, ewes, and rams of all colours, for the native sheep of that country are of different colours, like the horses in Spain. All this flock was the property of the Sun. They took a black lamb, for among the Indians this colour was preferred for the sacrifices, as more sacred. For they said that a black beast was black all over, while a white one, though its body might be white, always had a black nose, which was a defect, and caused it to be less perfect than a black beast. For this reason also, the Kings generally dressed in black, and their mouming was the natural colour of the wool, which they call grey.

This first sacrifice of a black lamb was made to prognosticate the omens of the festival. For they almost always sacrificed a lamb before undertaking any act either of peace or war, in order to see, by examining the heart and lungs, whether it was acceptable to the Sun, that is to say, whether it would be successful or the reverse. In order to seek an omen to tell them whether a harvest would be good; for some crops they used a lamb, for others a ram, for others a sterile ewe; but they never killed a fruitful sheep even to eat, until it was past bearing.

They took the lamb or sheep, and placed it with the head towards the east. They did not tie its feet, but three or four Indians held it, and it was cut open on the left side while still alive. They then forced their hands in, and pulled out the heart with the lungs and gullet up to the mouth, and the whole had to be taken out entire, without being cut.

If the lungs were palpitating, or had not ceased to live as they call it, the augury was looked upon as most fortunate. If this omen appeared, they took no note of others that might appear of an opposite character. For they said that the excellence of this lucky omen would overcome the evil of all contrary signs. They then took the entrails, blew air into them, and fastened up the mouth, or held it tight with their hands. Presently they began to watch the ways by which the air entered and distended the veins and arteries. If they were very full of air, it was looked upon as a good omen. They had other ways of seeking auguries of which I took no note, but I remember having seen these two methods practised on two occasions when I was a child. I went into a yard on one occasion, where some old unbaptised Indians were performing a sacrifice, not of the Raymi, for that festival had been abolished before I was born, but for some special purpose, in order to watch the omens. With this object they sacrificed lambs and sheep, as on the feast of Raymi, for their special sacrifices were performed in imitation of those at the great festivals.

It was considered a very bad omen if the beast rose on its feet while they were opening its side, in spite of those who held it; or if the entrails broke and did not come out whole. It was also an evil sign if the lungs or heart were torn or bruised in being pulled out; and there were other signs which, as I have said, I neither inquired about nor took note of. I remember this because I heard the Indians, who made the sacrifice, asking each other concerning the bad or evil omens, and they did not mind me because I was but a child.

To return to the solemnities of the Raymi. If the sacrifice of the lamb did not furnish good auguries, they made another sacrifice of a sheep, and if this was also unpropitious they offered up another. But, even if the third sacrifice was unlucky, they did not desist from celebrating the festival, though they did so with inward sorrow and misgiving, believing that their father, the Sun, was enraged against them for some fault or negligence that they must have unintentionally committed against his service.

They feared that cruel wars, failure of crops, diseases in their flocks, and other misfortunes might befall them. But when the omens were propitious, their joy was very great with which they celebrated the festival, as they looked forward to future good fortune.

After the sacrifice of the lamb, they brought a great quantity of lambs and sheep for a general sacrifice, and they did not cut these open while they were alive, but beheaded them first. The blood and hearts of all these, as well as of the first lamb, were preserved and offered to the Sun, and the bodies were burnt until they were converted to ashes.

It was necessary that the fire for the sacrifice should be new, and given by the hand of the Sun, as they expressed it. For this purpose they took a large bracelet, called chipana (like those they usually wear on the left thumb). This was held by the high priest. It was larger than usual, and had on it a highly polished concave plate, about the diameter of an orange. They put this towards the Sun, at an angle, so that the reflected rays might concentrate on one point, where they had placed a little cotton well pulled out, for they did not know how to make tinder; but the cotton was soon lighted in the natural way. With this fire, thus obtained from the hands of the Sun, they consumed the sacrifice, and roasted all the meat on that day. Portions of the fire were then conveyed to the temple of the Sun, and to the convent of virgins, where they were kept in all the year, and it was an evil omen if they were allowed to go out. If on the eve of the festival, which was the time when they made the preparations for the sacrifice, there was no sun wherewith to light the new fire, they obtained it by means of two thin cylindrical sticks, about the girth of a man's finger, and half a vara long, which they rubbed together. They give the name of Vyaca both to the sticks and to the act of obtaining fire from them, the same word serving both for a noun and a verb. The Indians use these sticks instead of flint and steel, and they travel with them, so as to have the means of making a fire at their sleeping places, when in an uninhabited region. I have often seen this when I have made a journey with the Indians, and the shepherds make use of sticks for the same purpose.

They looked upon it as a bad omen to light the fire for the festival in this way, saying that, as the Sun refused to kindle the flame with his own hand, he must be angry with them. All the meat for the feast was roasted in public, in the two squares, and it was distributed amongst all those who were present at the feast, whether Yncas, Curacas, or common people. And each received a piece of the bread called Canca with the meat. This was the first dish in their grand and solemn banquet. Afterwards they received a great quantity of eatables, which were eaten without drinking; for it was the universal custom of the Indians of Peru not to drink while they were eating.

From what has been related, the assertion made by some Spaniards may have arisen that the Yncas and their vassals communicated like Christians. We have described the custom of the Indians, and each reader can make out the similitude as he pleases.

After the eating was over, they brought liquor in great quantity, for this was one of the most prevalent vices among the Indians. But at the present day, through the mercy of God and the good example which has been set them in this particular by the Spaniards, no Indian can get drunk without being despised and reviled by his fellows. If the Spaniards had set a like example as regards other vices, they would have been apostolic preachers of the gospel.

The Ynca, seated in his golden chair, which was placed on a platform of the same metal, sent to the members of the tribes called Hanan Cuzco and Hurin Cuzco, desiring them to drink, in his name, with the most distinguished Indians belonging to other nations. First, they invited the captains who had shown valour in war, who, even when they were not lords of vassals, were for their bravery preferred to Curacas. But if a Curaca, besides being a lord of vassals, was also a captain in the wars, they did him honour both on the one account and on the other. Next the Ynca ordered the Curacas living in the vicinity of Cuzco, to be invited to drink, being those whose ancestors the first Ynca Manco Ccapac had reduced to his service. These chiefs, owing to the great privilege of bearing the name of Ynca, which that Prince had granted them, were looked upon as nobles of the highest rank next to the Yncas of the blood royal, and before all the chiefs of other tribes. For those kings never thought of diminishing in the smallest degree any privilege or favour that their ancestors had granted to any of their vassals, but on the contrary confirmed and increased them.

In these drinking bouts that the Indians had with each other, it must be understood that they all held their cups touching each other, two and two, and whether large or small, they were always of the same size and shape, and of the same metal, whether gold, silver or wood. This custom was enforced that each might drink the same quantity. He who gave an invitation to drink carried the two cups in his hands, and if the invited person was of lower rank he was given the cup in the left hand, if of equal or higher rank, the cup in the right; and with more or less ceremony according to the position in life of one and the other. Then they both drank together, and, the person inviting to drink, having received back his cup, returned to his place. On these occasions the first invitation was from a superior to his inferior, in token of favour and kindness. Afterwards the inferior invited his superior, as an acknowledgment of his vassalage and duty.

In observing this custom, the Ynca first sent an invitation to his vassals, in each nation preferring the captains before those who were not warriors. The Ynca who took the invitation said to the invited person:-"The sole Ynca sends me to invite you to drink, and I come to drink with you in his name." The captain or Curaca then took the cup with much reverence, raised his eyes to the Sun, as though he would give thanks for so undeserved a favour conferred by his son, and having drunk, he returned the cup to the Ynca without another word, only making signs of adoration with his hands and kissing the air with his lips.

And it must be understood that the Ynca did not send invitations to drink to all the Curacas (though he did so to all captains) but only to a select number, who were most worthy and who were most devoted to the public good. For this was the mark at which they all shot, as well the Ynca as the Curacas and the ministers of peace and war. The rest of the Curacas were invited to drink by the same Yncas who brought the cups, but in their own names and not in that of the Ynca, which satisfied them, because the invitation came from one who was a child of the Sun, like their king.

After the first invitation to drink, the captains and Curacas of all the nations returned the challenges in the order that they had received them, some to the Ynca himself, and the others to his relations, according as the first invitation had been received. The Ynca was approached without a word, and merely with the signs of adoration I have already described. He received them with much condescension, and took the cups they presented, but as he could not, nor was it lawful for him to drink of them all, he merely put them to his lips, drinking a little from all of them, from some more, from others less, according to the favour he wished to show to their owners, which was regulated by their rank and merit. And he ordered the attendants, who were all Yncas by privilege, to drink for him with those captains and Curacas; who having done so, returned the cups.

The Curacas held these cups in great veneration as sacred things, because the sole Ynca had touched them with his hands and lips. They never drank out of them again, nor touched them, but looked upon them as idols fit to be worshipped, in memory of their having been touched by the Ynca. Certainly nothing can show more than this how great was the love and veneration, both internal and outward, that these Indians felt for their kings.

The invitation and the return challenge to drink having been observed, all returned to their places. Presently the dances and songs began, in different fashions, and with the several insignia, masks, and dresses used by each nation. While the singing and dancing continued they did not leave off drinking, the Yncas and

Curacas inviting each other, according to their special friendships, or to the nearness of their places of residence.

The celebration of the feast of Raymi lasted for nine days, during which time there was abundance of eating and drinking, and such rejoicing as each person could show. But the sacrifices for observing omens were only made on the first day. As soon as the nine days were over the Curacas returned to their lands with the permission of the King, very joyful and contented at having celebrated the principal feast of their god the Sun. When the King was occupied in war or in visiting his dominions, he celebrated the feast in the place where he happened to be, but not with so much solemnity as when he was at Cuzco; while the Ynca governor, the High Priest, and others of the blood royal who remained behind, took care to celebrate it in the capital. On those occasions the Curacas assembled in the provinces, each one going to the feast which was held nearest to the place of his abode.

PACHACUTEC
(Ibid., pp. 201-210.)

THE YNCA PACHACUTEC, being now old, resolved to rest and not to make further conquests; for he had increased his empire until it was more than one hundred and thirty leagues from north to south, and in width from the snowy chain of the Andes to the sea, being sixty leagues from east to west in some places, and seventy in others, more or less. He now devoted himself to the confirmation of the laws of his ancestors, and to the enactment of new laws for the common good.

He founded many towns in those lands which by industry and by means of the numerous irrigation channels he caused to be made, were converted from sterile and uncultivated wilds into fruitful and rich districts.

He built many temples of the Sun in imitation of that of Cuzco, and many convents of virgins. He ordered many store-houses on the royal roads to be repaired, and houses to be built where the Yncas might lodge when travelling.

He also caused store-houses to be built in all villages, large or small, where supplies might be kept for succouring the people in time of scarcity, and he ordered these depots to be filled from the crops of the Ynca and of the Sun. In short, it may be said that he completely reformed the empire, as well as regards their vain religion, which he provided with new rites and ceremonies, destroying the numerous idols of his vassals, as by enacting new laws and regulations for the daily and moral life of the people, forbidding the abuses and barbarous customs to which the Indians were addicted before they were brought under his rule.

He also reformed the army in such fashion as proved him to be as great a captain as he was a king and a ruler; and he increased the honours and favours shown to those who distinguished themselves in war. He especially favoured and enlarged the great city of Cuzco, enriching it with new edifices and a larger population. He ordered a palace to be built for himself near the schools founded by his great grandfather Ynca Rocca. On account of these deeds, as well as for his amiable disposition and benignant government, he was loved and worshipped as another Jupiter. He reigned, according to the accounts of the Indians, more than fifty years, and some say more than sixty years. He lived in much peace and tranquillity, being alike beloved and obeyed, and at the end of this long time he died. He was universally lamented by all his vassals, and was placed among the number of their gods, as were the other Kings Yncas, his ancestors. He was embalmed, according to their custom, and the mourning, sacrifices and burial ceremonies lasted for a year.

He left as his heir the Ynca Yupanqui, who was his son by the Ccoya Anahuarque, his legitimate wife and sister. He left more than three hundred other sons and daughters, and some even say that, judging from his long life and the number of his wives, he must have had four hundred either legitimate or illegitimate children; and though this is a great many, the Indians say that it was few for such a father.

The Spanish historians confuse these two Kings, father and son, giving the names of both to one. The father was named Pachacutec. The name Ynca was common to all, for it was their title from the days of the first Ynca, called Manco Ccapac. In our account of the life of Lloque Yupanqui we described the meaning of the word Yupanqui, which word was also the name of this King, and combining the two names, they formed Ynca Yupanqui, which title was applied to all the Kings Yncas, so that Yupanqui ceased to be a special name. These two names are equivalent to the names Caesar Augustus, given to all the Emperors. Thus the Indians, in recounting the deeds of their Kings, and calling them by their names, would say, Pachacutec Ynca Yupanqui. The Spaniards understood that this was one King, and they do not admit the son and successor of Pachacutec, who was called Ynca Yupanqui, taking the two titles as his special name, and giving the same name to his own eldest son. But the Indians, to distinguish him from his father, called the latter Tupac (which means 'He who shines') Ynca Yupanqui. He was father of Huayna Ccapac Ynca Yupanqui, and grandfather of Huascar Ynca Yupanqui; and so all the other Yncas may be called by these titles. I have said this much to enable those who read this history to avoid confusion.

The Father Blas Valera, speaking of this Ynca, says as follows: "The Ynca Huiraccocha being dead and worshipped among the Indians as a god, his son, the great Titu, with surname of Manco Ccapac, succeeded him. This was his name until his father gave him that of Pachacutec, which means 'Reformer of the World.' That title was confirmed afterwards by his distinguished acts and sayings, insomuch that his first name was entirely forgotten. He governed his empire with so much industry, prudence and resolution, as well in peace as in war, that not only did he increase the boundaries of all the four quarters, called Ttahuantin suyu, but also he enacted many laws, all which have been confirmed by our Catholic Kings, except those relating to idolatry and to forbidden degrees of marriage. This Ynca above all things ennobled and increased, with great privileges, the schools that were founded in Cuzco by the King Ynca Rocca. He added to the number of the masters, and ordered that all the lords of vassals and captains and their sons, and all the Indians who held any office, should speak the language of Cuzco; and that no one should receive any office or lordship who was not well acquainted with it. In order that this useful law might have full effect, he appointed very learned masters for the sons of the princes and nobles, not only for those in Cuzco, but also for those throughout the provinces, in which he stationed masters that they might teach the language of Cuzco to all who were employed in the service of the state. Thus it was that in the whole empire of Peru one language was spoken, although now (owing to negligence) many provinces, where it was understood, have entirely lost it, not without great injury to the preaching of the gospel. All the Indians who, by obeying this law, still retain a knowledge of the language of Cuzco, are more civilised and more intelligent than the others.

"This Pachacutec prohibited any one, except princes and their sons, from wearing gold, silver, precious stones, plumes of feathers of different colours, nor the wool of the vicuña, which they weave with admirable skill. He permitted the people to be moderately ornamented on the first days of the month, and on some other festivals. The tributary Indians still observe this law, and content themselves with ordinary clothes, by which they avoid much vice which gay clothing is apt to cause. But the Indians, who are servants to Spaniards, and those who live in Spanish cities, are very extravagant in this particular, and do much harm alike to their pockets and consciences. This Ynca also ordered that great frugality should be observed in eating, although in drinking more freedom was allowed, both among the princes and the common people. He ordained that there should be special judges to try the idle, and desired that all should be engaged in work of some kind, either in serving their parents or masters, or in the service of the state; so much so, that even boys and girls of from five to seven years of age were given something to do suitable to their years. The blind, lame, and dumb, who could use their hands, were employed in some kind of work, and the aged were sent to scare the birds from the crops, and were supplied with food and clothing from the public store-houses. In order that labour might not be so continuous as to become oppressive, the Ynca ordained that there should be three holidays every month, in which the people should divert themselves with various games. He also commanded that there should be three fairs every month, when the labourers in the field should come to the market and hear anything that the Ynca or his Council might have ordained. They called these assemblies Catu, and they took place on the holidays.

"The Ynca also made a law that every province should have a fixed boundary enclosing the forests, pastures, rivers, lakes, mountains, and lands for tillage; all which should belong to that province and be within its jurisdiction in perpetuity. No Governor or Curaca could diminish or divide or appropriate to his own use any portion; but the land was divided according to a fixed rule which was defined by the same law for the common good, and the special benefit of the inhabitants of the province. The royal estates and those of the Sun were set apart, and the Indians had to plough, sow, and reap the crops, as well on their own lands as on those of the State. Hence it will be seen that it is false, what many have asserted, that the Indians had no proprietary right in the land. For this division was not made with reference to proprietary right, but for the common and special work to be expended upon the land. It was a very ancient custom among the Indians to work together not only on public lands, but also on their own, and with this view they measured the land, that each might complete such portion as he was able. The whole population assembled, and first worked their own lands in common, each one helping his neighbours, and then they began upon the royal estates; and the same practice was followed in sowing and in reaping. Almost in the same way they built their houses. The Indian who required a house went to the Council to appoint a day when it should be built, the inhabitants with one accord assembled to assist their neighbour, and thus the house was completed. The Ynca approved of this custom, and confirmed it by law. To this day many villages of Indians observe this law, and help each other with Christian charity; but avaricious men, who think only of themselves, do themselves harm and their neighbours no good.

"In fine, this King, with the advice of his Council, made many laws, rules, ordinances, and customs for the good of the people in numerous provinces. He also abolished many others which were detrimental either to the public peace or to his sovereignty. He also enacted many statutes against blasphemy, patricide, fratricide, homicide, treason, adultery, child-stealing, seduction, theft, arson; as well as regulations for the ceremonies of the temple. He confirmed many more that had been enacted by the

Yncas his ancestors; such as that sons should obey and serve their fathers until they reached the age of twenty-five, that none should marry without the consent of the parents, and of the parents of the girl; that a marriage without this consent was invalid and the children illegitimate; but that if the consent was obtained afterwards the children then became legitimate. This Ynca also confirmed the laws of inheritance to lordships according to the ancient customs of each province; and he forbade the judges from receiving bribes from litigants. This Ynca made many other laws of less importance, which I omit, to avoid prolixity. Further on I shall relate what laws he made for the guidance of judges, for the contracting of marriages, for making wills, and for the army, as well as for reckoning the years. In our time the Viceroy, Don Francisco de Toledo, changed or revoked many laws and regulations made by this Ynca; and the Indians, admiring his absolute power, called him the second Pachacutec, for they said he was the Reformer of the first Reformer. Their reverence and veneration for this Ynca was so great that to this day they cannot forget him."

Down to this point is from what I found amongst the torn papers of Father Blas Valera. That which he promises to write further on, touching the judges, marriages, wills, the army, and the reckoning of the year, is lost, which is a great pity. On another leaf I found part of the sententious sayings of this Ynca Pachacutec, which are as follows:--

"When subjects, captains and Curacas, cordially obey the King, then the kingdom enjoys perfect peace and quiet.

"Envy is a worm that gnaws and consumes the entrails of the envious.

"He that envies and is envied, has a double torment.

"It is better that others should envy you for being good, than that you should envy others, you yourself being evil.

"He that envies another, injures himself.

"He that envies the good, draws evil from them for himself, as does the spider in taking poison from flowers.

"Drunkenness, anger and madness go together; only the first two are voluntary and to be removed, while the last is perpetual.

"He that kills another without authority or just cause, condemns himself to death.

"He that kills his neighbour must of necessity die; and for this reason the ancient Kings, our ancestors, ordained that all homicides should be punished by a violent death, a law which we confirm afresh.

"Under no circumstances should thieves be tolerated, who, being able to gain a livelihood by honest labour and to possess it by a just right, wish to have more by robbing and stealing. It is very just that he who is a thief should be put to death.

"Adulterers, who destroy the peace and happiness of others, ought to be declared thieves, and condemned to death without mercy.

"The noble and generous man is known by the patience he shows in adversity.

"Impatience is the sign of a vile and base mind, badly taught and worse accustomed.

"When subjects do their best to obey without any hesitation, kings and governors ought to treat them with liberality and kindness; but when they act otherwise, with rigour and strict justice, though always with prudence.

"Judges who secretly receive gifts from suitors ought to be looked upon as thieves, and punished with death as such.

"Governors ought to attend to two things with much attention. The first is, that they and their subjects keep and comply exactly with the laws of their king. The second, that they consult with much vigilance and care, touching the common and special affairs of their provinces. The man who knows not how to govern his house and family, will know much less how to rule the state. Such a man should not be preferred above others.

"The physician herbalist that is ignorant of the virtues of herbs, or who, knowing the uses of some, has not attained a knowledge of all, understands little or nothing. He ought to work until he knows all, as well the useful as the injurious plants, in order to deserve the name he pretends to.

"He who attempts to count the stars, not even knowing how to count the marks and knots of the 'quipus,' ought to be held in derision."

These are the sayings of Ynca Pachacutec. He speaks of the marks and knots of the accounts because, as they had neither letters for writing nor figures for ciphering, they kept their accounts by means of marks and knots.

THREE INCA PRAYERS

From: Ancient Civilizations of the Andes by Philip Ainsworth Means, New York: Charles Scribner's Sons, 1931, pp. 437-439

TO VIRACOCHA

Viracocha, Lord of the Universe!
Whether male or female,
at any rate commander of heat and reproduction,
being one who,
even with His spittle, can work sorcery,
Where art Thou?
Would that Thou wert not hidden from this son of Thine!
He may be above;
He may be below;
or, perchance, abroad in space.
Where is his mighty judgment-seat?
Hear me!
He may be spread abroad among the upper waters;
or, among the lower waters and their sands
He may be dwelling.
Creator of the world,
Creator of man,
great among my ancestors,
before Thee my eyes fail me,
though I long to see Thee;
for, seeing Thee,
knowing Thee,
learning from Thee,
understanding Thee,

I shall be seen by Thee,
and Thou wilt know me.
The Sun--the Moon;
The Day--the Night;
Summer--Winter;
not in vain,
in orderly succession,
do they march to their destined place,
to their goal.
They arrive
wherever
Thy royal staff
Thou bearest.
Oh! Harken to me,
listen to me,
let it not befall
that I grow weary
and die.

TO VIRACOCHA

O conquering Viracocha!
Ever-present Viracocha!
Thou who art without equal upon the earth!
Thou who art from the beginnings of the world until its end!
Thou gavest life and valour to men, saying,
"Let this be a man."
And to woman, saying,
"Let this be a woman."
Thou madest them and gavest them being.
Watch over them, that they may live in health and in peace.
Thou who art in the highest heavens,
and among the clouds of the tempest,
grant them long life,
and accept this our sacrifice,

O Creator.

TO PACHACAMAC

O Pachacamac!
Thou who hast existed from the beginning,
Thou who shalt exist until the end,
powerful but merciful,
Who didst create man by saying,
"Let man be,"
Who defendest us from evil,
and preservest our life and our health,
art Thou in the sky or upon the earth?
In the clouds or in the deeps?
Hear the voice of him who implores Thee,
and grant him his petitions.
Give us life everlasting,
preserve us, and accept this our sacrifice.

www.ingramcontent.com/pod-product-compliance
Lightning Source LLC
Chambersburg PA
CBHW051553010526
44118CB00022B/2694